Night Drives

Samantha Camargo

Contents

Let's go on a night drive..

Windows
Down

Some days you wake up and you feel like a new person.. and it's scary because you don't know who you are anymore..

and you're not sure if you've lost yourself or if you've finally found yourself.

I miss who I used to be.
I miss being full of energy.
I miss being excited
to get out of bed in the morning.
I miss being pulled by my vision.
I miss feeling good in my body.
But most of all, I miss
loving myself enough
to take care of myself.

I don't know what happened
to my drive and determination,
my mindset, my energy, and
the confidence I had in myself..

..the love I had for others, myself,
and the love I had for life..

But.. I know I haven't lost it;
I know it's still somewhere inside of me.
It has just been buried beneath all the
3 a.m. thoughts I let inside, and let consume me.
But it hurts too much now, the weight of it all..
and I think I am finally ready to let go of the
heavy thoughts and feel like myself again.

You put on layer
after layer.

Covered yourself up
so carefully.

And now you're safe.
No one can hurt you now.

But no one can love you either
because you won't let anyone
see past the surface.

You won't let anyone in.

I'm not sure what I'm afraid of more.
Feeling alone or letting people in.

If we all want to love someone,
then why is it so hard to love ourselves?

You want so badly to love someone,
to give them all of your heart,
to try to make them happy
when they are sad,
to wipe away their tears
and tell them everything will be alright.
To be there for them, always..
but you forgot to do all of this for yourself.

Please remember to love yourself too.

Sometimes people will try to give you
some of their anger, their sadness,
their fear, or their guilt because
it's too much for them to bear alone.

You need to remember, you do not have
to take what they are trying to give you.
You have a choice.

Instead, you could offer them
some of your kindness,
your understanding,
your compassion,
your love..

All you want is to be left alone, and it's not until everyone's gone that you realize what you really wanted was to be able to connect with someone.

His smiles were lies
He got so good at hiding
his tears disappeared
before they left his eyes.

If you tell them to open up,
be there for them when they do.

It hurts,
opening up and tearing down your wall..
only to find yourself facing another wall.

So many of us have been taught to be people pleasers, but maybe that's why so many of us are so unhappy.

Because we know how to make others happy, but not ourselves.

Boys are told "don't cry"
and then he doesn't
and we wonder why

Men are told "Be a man. Don't cry.
That's a sign of weakness."
when it's really a sign of being alive.
Men are taught to hide
to be emotionless
to be dead inside.
They act cold and numb
and we wonder "Why?
Where are.. What happened to..
all the nice guys?"
They act heartless and distant
and the question
remains persistent..
Why do we tell them
to be indifferent
and then get angry
when they listen?

Crying is not weakness; it is vulnerability. It is strength. To feel unbearable pain, so much pain that your body needs to release it, and to be able to keep going after

...that is strength not weakness.

And it was easier
for them to be angry
than to be sad,
but they didn't realize
all the anger
caused more
sadness.

*Don't fight someone who
is at war with themselves.*

You see her mask,
her flawless art,
but you don't see
all the times
she's put herself
together
and fallen apart.
You don't see
her pain,
her scars.

Who ever told you that you were not enough?
Whoever they were, they did not know you at all..
because if they did, they would've seen the spark
in your eyes, the light in your soul, and the magic
in your laughter. They would've seen the dark
times that you've been through and how your light
now shines brighter in spite of it. They would've
seen all of your human "flaws" and characteristics,
the past experiences you've been through and
"mistakes" you've made, and they would know that
you are much more than all of that.
They would've seen that you've always been enough,
even when they said you weren't.

They would have seen you.

Just because you don't understand someone else's pain doesn't mean their pain isn't real.

When someone says they are tired, please don't make them feel as if they have no reason for being tired. They could be tired emotionally or mentally. They could be tired in ways you can't even see or in ways you've never even felt...

and it's even more tiring trying to explain that.

I want to see you again.. and I want to be able to hold you again. Even if it's just in my dreams. But I haven't been able to sleep, and when I do, I wake up not able to remember what I dreamt about. All I remember is that you are gone all over again.

It's a cycle. You're hurt and you hurt others, but you end up hurting yourself even more.

*In relationships, souls love and connect;
egos argue and hurt each other.*

Caring is not a weakness. It takes strength to care.. and it takes courage to care in a world that wants you to stay indifferent.

Be kind and lift others up.

If you treat someone as if they're stupid and worthless, that is the only way you will ever see them. You are in no way helping them. Your words are not toughening them up or building character. You are bringing them down and slowly breaking them; you are tearing their soul apart.. and when they do grow from this experience, it will not be because of you. They will grow stronger because they chose to love themselves in a way you never could, in a way you were never able to love yourself.

If someone says you're not enough
have compassion
because they've been taught
their worth is conditional

You know how we can be so hard on ourselves and we can look in the mirror and can pick out every physical "flaw" we have? And how our "flaws" look so major and awful and as if it's the first thing people will notice about us? But have you ever thought of it this way? When you look at people do you notice a lot of flaws on them? *I think most of us don't. I think most of us care more about what's inside of people rather than what's on the outside.* When you're talking to someone are you looking at them and noticing their "flaws" or are you listening to what they are saying, and thinking of how kind they are or how funny or caring they are? When you pass by a stranger, do you notice their "flaws" or are you too busy noticing their smile? Are you left with impressions of people's "flaws" or are you left with the feeing they gave you? How they made you laugh or how they made you smile or how they made you remember you're not alone?

If you have a hard time appreciating, loving, and accepting how you look on the outside, focus on loving what's on the inside... because that's what really matters.

If you can start with loving who you are on the inside, then one day you will also be able to love who you are on the outside.

*And maybe one day
he will stop pushing others away.
Maybe one day he will finally feel
he deserves to be loved*

I know something happened that made you stop
loving. I don't think you were even aware of it.
But something happened and you slowly stopped
loving. Quietly and without even realizing it, you
tucked away your heart behind layers of
protection. So tightly wrapped that it could hardly
beat, and the light in your eyes began to fade.
But I know that one day, you will be ready to start
loving again.. and your heart will break free
from your own lock and key
and the spark in your eyes
will shine again.

It's scary how happy I get around you.
I spent so long learning how to be happy
on my own.. and I promised myself
I would never lose that.

That's great that you're happy
when you're with them.

But remember,
you don't need them
in order to be happy.

*Have you ever felt like
no one really sees you..
and even if you screamed,
they wouldn't hear you?*

I was lost and scared.. and the fear didn't come from being lost. I was afraid I wouldn't care enough to find my way back, back to who I was before I let myself begin to fade away.

—

They quickly judged her for being heartless,
but what they didn't realize was she felt empty
and didn't feel as if she had any love left to give..
and that she had once cared "too much",
so now she protected herself by acting as if
she didn't care at all.

He laughed when he was sad, when he was angry, when he was scared. He laughed and made it easy for you to walk by as if you hadn't noticed the emptiness in his eyes..

Every time something triggers your mind to replay everything that happened, everything you were trying to forget.. and it takes your breath away and you feel as if your heart is about to leave your chest, please remember to breathe.

Breathe in. Breathe out.

Feel your heart beating and feel the presence inside of you. Each beat is carrying you through this. You are getting stronger.. and you will get through this, just as you always have.

How many times have you cried yourself to sleep
and woke up from a nightmare
only to find it wasn't just a dream?

You know how sometimes you aren't even aware you have a paper cut until you use hand sanitizer?

Then all of a sudden, it hurts so much, but a second ago you had no idea the cut even existed.

I think healing is like that.

Sometimes you don't even know there's a part of you that's still hurt until something comes along that forces you to become aware of it, forcing you to deal with it.

Maybe their soul is buried too deep they think they can't feel it anymore. Maybe their thoughts are too loud they can't hear their soul even though their soul is trying to reach them.

He didn't feel good enough..
so he cheated on her
Her self-worth shattered..
she said, "love doesn't matter,"
took another boy's heart
and tore it apart
He said, "should've known
from the start.."
broke another girl's heart
told her, "love isn't real
you can't trust how you feel
and hearts don't mend"
This cycle of pain
drives them all insane
When does it end
when does it end
does it end?

There's a lot of pressure from society to hurry up and find a partner, but isn't it more important to find ourselves first?

You said
you did love me,
before I changed.
But I didn't change;

I finally gathered
the strength
to be vulnerable,
the courage
to reveal myself.

So I guess,
you never loved me.
You loved who
you thought
I was.

They say to open up.

Be vulnerable.
But when his
walls are down,
and they see
his pain,
his scars
and blood,
his open wound...

they close up.

He asked her
to give him a hand
but she could not
her hands were full,
holding herself together

When I haven't been sleeping well, I feel so sad during the day.. and I wonder, does everyone feel this sad when they are tired?

Or is it because I don't have the energy to fight off my own thoughts?

Because right now, I feel like there's so much sadness inside of me, and I don't know how to get rid of it.

-but I will find a way. I will not let it consume me.

Sometimes people think I'm heartless and that I don't feel anything. It's not that I don't feel anything. I actually feel everything... and sometimes it's too much and I just need to shut it off for a little while so that I can keep going. If I ever seem as if I don't care, it's because I care too much... more than I can handle.

No one knows how many times I've thought
of leaving this body. But, I'm still here.. and I'm
hanging on because I want to go exploring while
the sun is rising and feel the sun beaming down
on my face and the wind brushing against my
skin. I want to lie on the beach with the sand
encompassing my body as the sun is slowly
setting and there's nowhere else I need to be.
I want to experience those moments when
it feels as if time is standing still;

There have been so many times
I've wanted to leave this body,
but maybe it's not my body
I wanted to leave,
but my mind.

You've made so much progress in the past few months and you've worked so hard. These past few days of you doing "nothing" is really nothing compared to how much progress you've already made. Don't be so hard on yourself.

-Tomorrow is a new day.

His dreams scared them. They didn't want to hear that he believed he could make his dreams a reality. They didn't want him to go after his dreams because if he succeeded, if he achieved his dreams, it would mean they could have lived their dreams too, if they had only dared to try.

Someone asked you what you're so afraid of,
and you realized you really don't know and that
terrified you because it made you think maybe
you do know, but you're so afraid of it that
your mind won't even let you face it.

But if you keep your fears locked up,
hidden from view, how can you ever
free yourself from them?

*You look in their eyes
and hope they will find
you're screaming inside*

If you've never felt like going to sleep and
never waking up, then you don't understand
how waking up can be the hardest thing
for someone.

If you've never felt what it's like to want to
stop breathing, you don't understand how
someone can be brave by doing nothing else
but breathe today, nothing else but stay alive.

It may seem as if they are doing so little.
It may seem as if they are doing nothing.
But it's a lot.

It's everything.

Don't be so hard on others.
Have some compassion.

I didn't need you.

I could handle it on my own.
But, I really wanted you. I wanted you to be here.
I wanted you to look me in my eyes and be able
to see how much I'm hurting, even if I tried to
hide it. I wanted to hear your voice whisper in my
ear that I'm not alone. I wanted the comfort of
your arms. I wanted your presence.
I didn't need you..

but I wanted you.

And I'm not sure if the pain is going away or if I'm just getting better at distracting myself from it

Maybe it affected me more than I thought it did.
Maybe I bottled it up inside, tried to put myself
back together as if nothing happened,
as if it didn't bother me.

But I can feel it now.

It's not good to bottle things up inside
because eventually
you will feel as if you're drowning.

Allow yourself to feel what you are feeling
and then let it go otherwise it will add up and
weigh you down.

If I'm being honest, then yes. Yes, it hurt. I'm not going to pretend that it didn't. It wasn't the sharp, crushing pain that you feel in your chest when you can't stop crying and your whole body aches. It was more of a silent, dull pain. A pain that slowly crept in like a fog, suffocating my heart. Almost to the point where I couldn't feel anything at all. To the point where I started to feel numb. Fading.
I could feel myself going numb. And it was tempting. To feel nothing at all instead of feeling this pulsating pain.
But, I realized I didn't want my heart to go numb. I didn't want my heart to stop feeling. I could handle feeling this pain with each beat because as long as I felt it, it meant I was alive.
And as long as I was alive, even if it was painful in this moment, it meant that I had the chance to love again one day.

And that was enough to keep my heart beating

Sometimes people will stay quiet around you,
not because they have nothing to say,
but because they have learned that even if
they spoke to you, you wouldn't hear them.
You say you're there to listen..
and your ears are open, but your mind is not.

He wanted to be himself, but they wanted him to be "normal". They hated who he was, but he still loved them. He didn't want to see the look of disgust and hate in their eyes so he pretended he was something he wasn't to make them happy.

But you see, they said they loved him now, but he still saw the look of disgust and hate.. in his own eyes when he looked in the mirror, conditioned to believe who he truly was wasn't good enough to be loved.

Why is it more acceptable for us to focus on how we look than on how we treat others?

Comparing another person's pain to your own is not healthy. Saying that yours is worse or better doesn't help anyone. It's not a competition.

Everyone's pain is valid.

Be gentle with yourself. "Slacking off" did not erase all of the progress you've already made. You can begin again as many times as you'd like. Be excited to begin again. Be proud to begin again, no matter how many times you have to because with each time, it means you are getting closer and closer to achieving your goals.

Don't be afraid to begin again.

They judge you to distract themselves
from all the ways they judge themselves.

Being kind to others
does not make you "fake"
and being purposefully rude
doesn't make you "real".

Stop wondering why they didn't like you. Instead, spend that time learning to love yourself without needing validation.

They ask you why you never talk to them,
but when you try to talk, they don't listen..
and as time passes, you can't even
get the words out, only tears.

Just because something is considered "normal"
in a society, it doesn't make it okay.

It doesn't make it the most loving,
the most compassionate thing to do.

When you realize this..
what are you going to choose?

To contribute to cruelty because it's "normal" to?
Or to contribute kindness, compassion, and love?

What do you choose?

I can pretend I don't care really easily,
and I used to think this was a strength.
But now I think it's more of a weakness.

*–because I'm too afraid to let people see
how I truly feel.*

Torn between wanting to be open and vulnerable and honest and wanting to go back to what I'm comfortable with, hiding what I am feeling.

Have you ever shared something with someone and then wish you hadn't? You wish you hadn't been that honest and vulnerable with them and regret you let them see that part of you. But, try to remind yourself not to regret it. Not to regret being yourself. You deserve people in your life who don't make you feel as if you need to keep parts of yourself hidden. People who make you feel safe as you allow yourself to be vulnerable around them.

You deserve that.

Sometimes she hated her imagination for the same reason she loved it. For taking her out of the moment she was in and making her thoughts feel more real than reality.

And maybe it wasn't the dark you were afraid of, but being alone with the darkness of your own thoughts.

Sometimes when I'm going through something,
I don't tell anyone. And I know that's not healthy.
But then if I talk about it, then I have to admit
it's real... and I don't want it to be real.

You never really know how much space
someone takes up in your heart,
until they're gone
and you feel
a type of emptiness
you've never felt before.

But it was hard to let go of anger
Because if I did then sadness would come,
and I wouldn't have anything to stop myself
from feeling it.

When you guard your heart,
you think you are protecting yourself
from getting hurt,
but you are actually hurting yourself
the most
by imprisoning yourself.

And maybe they felt empty
because they knew
how to give love,
but they didn't know
how to accept it.

I feel so sad
I don't know where to put it.
I try to let it go with every
tear..
But I feel it everywhere
I can't find myself
here

Please don't chain a weight to my leg,
throw me in the ocean and then tell me to
"let it go" so I can swim back to the surface.

Do you think it's hard for some of us to open up to others, not because we are afraid they won't love us for who we are, but because deep down we think we don't deserve to be loved? ..and so we keep our guard slightly up, never allowing anyone to truly see us, never allowing ourselves to be loved for who we are.

You find it hard to believe when someone
tells you they love you, even after they've seen
all of you, inside and out,
and it's not because you are not loveable.

It's because it's taken you so long to learn
to love yourself and some days you still can't
feel love for yourself, so you can't see how
someone else could fall in love with you
so quickly and so unconditionally.

It hurts when someone talks about you behind your back, spreading lies.. but when someone you thought was your friend does it, your trust is gone and you're left with wondering why.

When something happens and it hurts me, I'm okay with being sad. I can deal with it because I know why I'm feeling that way. But being sad and not knowing why. That's the worst. Because when someone asks me what's wrong, I can't answer them because I don't even know myself.. and sometimes I just feel like crying, but force myself to hold it in because I can't let anyone see me cry. Because then they'll ask why... and I don't know why.

But I know things will get better.

Please don't say you "need" me.
Please don't tell me you only feel alive
when you're around me.
I don't want to be your only life source,
your only source of happiness.
Tell me you want me.
Tell me you want to share
your happiness with me.
But please don't say
that I am your everything,
the only reason
you wake up every morning.
I can't live with that pressure..
and you deserve to feel alive
every second of your life.

I think what happened was they were both looking for different things. He was looking for happiness from one source: her

And she was looking for happiness from every single thing she could in life because she knew what it was like to look for all of your happiness in one person.

Once they were gone, it would be hard to find.

If everyone comes into our lives for a reason, what is the reason for the ones we let into our lives only for them to leave?

Maybe it's not to show you that you are weak for letting someone in and caring so much for them. Maybe it's to show you how strong you are to have let down your guard to love someone...

and even though it felt as if they walked away with your heart, your heart is still beating.

Can you feel it?

It's stronger than it was before...
and it's never leaving.

Sometimes people won't understand how one person could affect you so much, could cause you so much pain, suffering, and heartache.

They may not understand how difficult it is to get over one person. But what they don't understand is that it's not always just one person. It is one person, but at the same time it's not just one; it's everyone who has ever made you feel as if you weren't enough, everyone who has ever made you question whether you deserve to be loved, everyone you've loved who didn't love you back.

But at the core of everything, maybe it hurts so intensely because this "one" person who broke your heart is actually you, by needing someone else's love and validation before giving yourself permission to love yourself and be happy on your own.

What if we feel so alone
because we're terrified of
being intimate with another,

especially ourselves?

*Falling for someone's looks
is not the same as falling
in love.*

She wanted to strip down to her soul
to feel the freedom of transparency.
But, she could not reveal herself
completely to others
because she was still learning
how to uncover the parts
she kept hidden even from herself.

I once told my friend that the hardest part was hiding it. Going to school and walking around as if everything was okay, looking straight ahead, trying to make it from one class to the next without looking anyone in the eyes so no one could see I'd been crying, and if they did, it would be easier for them to pretend they didn't.

I told them hiding it hurt the most... and they asked me, "then why did you hide it?" and to be honest, I don't know. It was a reflex to hide it.. to pretend everything was okay.. to pretend I was okay. Maybe I was scared of people finding out I wasn't as strong as I pretended to be, and maybe deep down, I was scared that if I let them see I was at my lowest, no one would care.

Everyone would just walk right by as if they didn't see me struggling to get up. And so even though it was the hardest thing for me to do, pretending was easy.

Pretending I wasn't broken was easier than the thought of being crushed as people walked right through me. It was easier to cover up than to expose myself for everyone to see, only to find no one really saw me.

– *it was easier to pretend*

You thought you covered yourself with a mask because you didn't want anyone to see you.

But it was really because you were tired of feeling the pain of staring at face after face and no one ever seeing you.

Do you ever wonder how many people think they know you, but if you were introduced to the person they think you are that person would be a stranger to you?

*She left him and she
knew she would miss him
but she didn't want to
miss herself anymore*

When you're in a relationship, I hope you never change who you are in hopes of trying to please your partner.

–because if you do, then who do they love? You? Or the person you think they want you to be?

She touched my hand like it meant something
she kissed my lips like it meant something
she held my heart like it meant something
but then she tore it apart like it
meant nothing

And maybe one day
when I hear your name,
it won't be your name anymore.
Maybe you won't come to mind
and it will be
just another name to me,
as it was before I met you...
and when I hear it,
maybe my heart won't sink.
And I won't wonder
if you ever think of me.

You know that one person whose attention you've been craving? That one person you're fixated on noticing you. What if the person you are truly wanting to notice you is not them but yourself? What if you are waiting for yourself to see yourself for who you really are? You are incredible beyond words and you deserve to be loved for exactly who you are right now. That person who you wish could see you, I mean really see you.. what if it's not their attention and love you are craving, but your own? Maybe it's easier to feel as if you are being denied the love you are seeking from another person than realizing you are denying it from yourself.

You don't need them to fall in love with you, in order to fall in love with yourself.

I find myself suffering because all I want is to be good enough for others, and I feel as if I never am. But when will I realize I only need to be "good enough" for myself? When will I be good enough for myself? When will I learn to love and accept myself? When will I stop this suffering, and finally find peace within myself?

You know how some people say,
"no one will ever love me"?

Well, that's not true. They feel that it's true, but it's not. People will love you, but if you don't love yourself, you won't be able to comprehend why they love you and you won't believe that they love you, so in your mind, "no one loves me and no one ever will" sounds like the truth, but it's actually a lie because people do love you. Just because you can't see it right now because you're so used to telling yourself no one ever will, doesn't mean they don't... because they do.

You are loved and always will be.

That person who is really kind to you
and truly believes in you is not "too kind".
It just seems like they are because other people
and our thoughts and beliefs about ourselves
can be so cruel.

He could've made a difference in the world. Instead, you told him over and over and over it wouldn't make a difference if he was gone from the world.

Making fun of someone
doesn't point out their insecurities;
it points out yours.

The thing I want most is connection,
so it scares me how easily I can disconnect.

*–and I wonder if it's because I don't believe
I am worthy of connection.*

Do you ever think maybe we spend too much time talking about others, judging others, and judging ourselves that we forget to talk within ourselves.. to self-reflect.. and so we stay stuck in the same patterns and we stunt our growth?

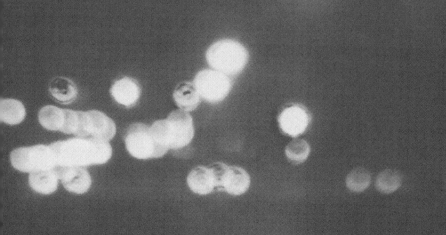

I forgive others so easily,
but I'm still learning how
to forgive myself.

Being fixated on being constantly happy and denying ourselves from feeling other emotions makes it seem like life is not good unless it's great.

Happiness is only an emotion.
Love is a constant.
There will always be
"highs and lows" in life;
it's unavoidable.
But no one can take
the love you feel
(for yourself,
for others,
for life)
away.

It can feel scary, but find the courage
to reach out to others.
How can you ever get through this
if you pretend you aren't even
going through anything
and that everything is okay?

It can feel terrifying, but find the strength
to let it out.
How can you let it go and move on
if you are still grasping it,
holding it all inside?

Even though it can be hard,
find a way to open up.
How can you expect to ever release
yourself from what you are going through
if you keep holding it in?

If you are feeling sad and your heart hurts or you can feel the ache in your chest from missing someone or you've been crying all day no more tears will come, and you can feel yourself becoming numb please know that *you are not alone.*

I know that sometimes it feels as if you're alone, and you feel like no one understands the pain you're feeling, but reach out to people and you'll find you're not alone. I know sometimes your mind makes you believe you're alone, but truly you are not. *Please know this.*

And please, when the wave comes, don't numb yourself. Feel the pain, the grief, the sadness. Don't numb yourself. Feel it and let it wash over you, but do not allow yourself to drown in it. There is nothing wrong with feeling these feelings. *You do not need to be happy all of the time, but you do deserve to be happy.*

So when you feel yourself fading, don't. Feel the ache in your chest and let it be a reminder that you are alive, and you still have the ability to feel. You may be feeling pain or grief or sadness right now, but soon you will be able to feel joy and bliss and happiness again. Soon, that emptiness you're feeling deep in your soul will be gone, replaced with so much love. *Please know that this is possible for you.*

Music Up

How do you let the poison out
..without hurting the ones you love?

Where do you release it?

Through the tip of a pen?
Through the breath of an exhale?

By an ocean while the sun is setting?
Along the road as you drive
with no destination in mind?

Where do you release it?

Do you ever look at old photos and think of how you look so happy?

The person in the photo didn't know what would happen in 2 days or a month or a year. They didn't even know what would happen the next day.

Things weren't "perfect" for them then and they didn't know what was coming next, but they were happy. And if you could be that happy then, maybe you could be that happy now.

All this time I've spent worrying,
I could've done all of the things
I worried I wouldn't have time to do.

Everyone told her that time heals all wounds. But to her, it felt as if time was standing still and the wound was getting deeper.

Maybe it wasn't time that healed. Maybe it was experience. Whether or not you allowed yourself out into the world after you'd been hurt. Making new memories to immerse yourself in instead of replaying the same ones that leave you feeling lifeless over and over. Filling yourself with life again, instead of waiting the rest of your life for time to heal you.

You're going to miss someone so much it hurts. You're going to get hurt and the pain will feel unbearable. It's going to be 3 in the morning, and you'll feel as if you can't take one more breath, but you breathe. You keep going. You grieve. You heal. You grow. You fall in love and you never give up.

Sometimes when you're healing
you don't know if it's getting worse
and you're breaking down
or if you're getting better
and about to break free.

The healing is going to hurt.
It's going to be hard.
You're going to wonder
if things are ever getting better.
You're going to struggle and cry
and wish it was over.
You might feel as if you are breaking..
but you are not.
The cycle is.
You are helping the healing
of generations of pain,
and this is why it hurts so much.
Don't give up.
Souls around the world
are rooting for you.
You are healing..
you are growing..
you are breaking
the cycle of pain.

I know that it might seem like all that surrounds you is darkness, but you are the light.. and maybe you can't see that now, but that's why I want to hand you a mirror, to help you see who you are, who you've always been.

Quiet all the thoughts that tell you you'll never
be enough, the thoughts that keep you up
at night, the thoughts that try to reach your heart
through their whispers, the thoughts that crawl
under your skin.

Silence them and tell me,
what does your soul say.

You are not hard to love.
It is so easy to love you.
When I look at you,
all I can feel is love.

-Who ever made you think
 loving you was hard?

I want to have that
"butterflies in my stomach" feeling
every morning as I wake up.
But, I don't want it to depend
on someone else.
I want to have that
exhilarating, exciting feeling
just for waking up,
realizing I have another day to live.
I want to have that fresh, blissful feeling
because I am alive
and I am in love with life.

Those songs that you find.. or maybe they find you.. and it makes you feel as if you've just found another part of your soul.. it makes you feel as if your soul is growing.

It makes you feel reconnected with who you are, and as if anything is possible.. you could be completely bare.. and vulnerable.. and no one is judging you..
and even if they were,
you wouldn't care.

Those songs that give you oxygen, the ones that make you feel as if you're taking your first breath over and over again.. those songs are important.

Those are your soul songs.
Listen to them.
They will nourish you.

It feels amazing to have people in your life who make you happy.. and just seeing them makes you smile. But, I hope you remember not to allow your happiness to rely on anyone. You should be one of the people in your life who makes you happy. That way you could be happy even when you're alone.

You look at someone and you can
see that they are capable.
You can see their potential.
You can see them achieving anything
they set their mind to.
You can see they have what it takes
inside of them to live their dreams.
But please remember to look at yourself,
and see all of this is also inside of you.

Remember to believe in yourself too.

"I want my life to mean something,"
he confided to her.
She reminded him, "it already does."

Stop with the idea in your head
that one day, when you are successful,
you will "be somebody".
You are just as important today
as you will be when you are successful.
Your life matters just as much now
as it will later.
Strive to become your best self.
Don't strive to be somebody.
You already are.
You just need to show up in your life.
Be present, and you will have arrived.

It's not too late. You still have time to remember who you truly are. To use your pain as a source of growth instead of a source of suffering.. and to start living the life you've always dreamed you'd one day live.

Stop pretending you're okay
with things you know in your soul
you are not okay with.

She tried so hard
to make everyone happy,
but she realized
she was forgetting someone:
herself

Don't make decisions
to try to please someone else
because once they're gone,
you'll be left living a life
you never truly wanted.

*How can you feel good if you continuously
do things that make you feel bad?*

We are all born somebody.
But as we grow up, we start to
bury ourselves with a mask..
and we go out trying to
make something of ourselves,
to "be somebody"..
forgetting what we buried.
Forgetting who we are.

Moments like this make me so grateful
I am alive to experience it,
to feel the air lightly brush my body,
as if to tell me that everything
will be okay, telling me to forget
my worries and just enjoy this moment
because this moment is enough,
this moment is all I need.

I want to spend my life
in my body, living,
not in my mind, worrying

Learn to care enough about yourself
to keep the promises you make to yourself.

Some days it will be hard for you to feel love for yourself, but those are the days you need to allow yourself to feel it the most.

She felt as if she was falling apart,
but something kept her together.
As she slowly breathed in,
and felt the beat of her heart,
she knew that with each beat,
there was a hidden promise
of a fresh start.

Her goal was to become so strong
that a few words could no longer
crush her soul.

I broke down,
but I am not
broken.

Your body will heal, the bags under your eyes
will go away, you'll be so happy you'll smile
and really mean it, and most of all,
your heart will feel full again.

– things will get better

I didn't realize it at the time, but I placed all
of my love in you, until it hurt, until my heart
felt it had nothing left to give. But, love is not what hurt.
Giving love was not what hurt. It was the absence of love
that hurt. I had given you all of my love, my whole heart
and left nothing for myself. I waited for you to give me a
piece
of yours and that is what hurt.

*-it hurt until I stopped waiting and found
the love I had longed for from you in myself.*

*Do you know how much strength he has
to feel things so deeply, every day
when he could numb himself
and look the other way*

You can't choose who you fall in love with.
It just happens.

But if they don't feel the same way,
you have a choice.

You can choose to leave your heart
with them, broken.. or you can choose
to take back the pieces and move on,
knowing that now, you have everything
you need to feel whole again.

I don't believe in wasted love.
Love is never wasted.
If you put love out there,
it makes a difference.
Love makes a difference.

Try not to get upset if someone doesn't believe you when you first tell them you love them. Try to understand that if someone doesn't love themselves, it can be hard for them to believe anyone else does. Be gentle with them. You can't make them love themselves. All you can do is love them and hope they realize they are loved. And hope that they fall in love with themselves just as you have fallen in love with them.

When I was younger, I believed if your heart was broken you needed to find someone to heal it.

Then I realized your heart can only be broken and healed by one person: you. You break your own heart every day when you deprive it of your own love, thinking you have to wait for the love from another to feel complete.

You heal it by giving love to yourself and not needing to receive love before *you can feel whole.*

Just be yourself and if you two connect then it will be a genuine connection.. and if you don't, at least you didn't lose the connection with who you are.

Remember to always be grateful for everyone in your life, not because you are afraid you will lose them one day, but because you are grateful to have them in your life now, and you don't want a day to go by where you don't realize how blessed you truly are.

She continued to surprise people.
As if they expected her
to remain the same,
to never change.
As if she was only allowed
to have one side of her.
They thought they knew
what she was capable of.
–but, she was capable
of so much more

If you ever look back and wonder where all your motivation, drive, and energy went, just remember that maybe you're too tired today, but one day, you can be like that again.

It's all still inside of you.

It doesn't matter how long you rest or how many times you keep getting up. What matters is that you don't give up on yourself. You are worth it. You are worth it, even when you don't feel as if you are.

Let's train our minds to look for
more reasons to keep going
rather than reasons to give up.

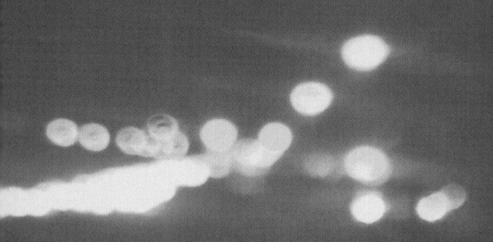

You are changing. You are growing.
But don't let your love for yourself change.

If you are waiting for someone to reassure you of your worth, isn't it because you feel as if you need confirmation?

Confirmation that you really are good enough. That you really are worthy. That you really are loveable. You feel as if you can finally approve of yourself once they approve of you first. You are looking for an external source of approval. But, doesn't it make sense to get the approval straight from the once source that matters? Yourself. Love yourself. Approve of yourself.

What could be more gratifying than telling yourself you approve of yourself and that you love yourself unconditionally instead of waiting for someone else to approve of you?

~~real~~ men ~~don't~~ cry
and don't let *anyone*
tell you otherwise.
"it's weak to feel"
..that's a lie
that only keeps us
feeling numb inside.
it takes strength to feel
when you're taught to hide

You don't have to pretend you're happy
when you're not.

You don't have to be happy all the time.

You don't have to smile
when you're hurting.

You don't have to hide your sadness.
Your sadness is not an inconvenience.
Your feelings are not an inconvenience.

We can't fix
each other
but we can
show each other
our souls were
never broken

Choose "I'll try again"
a million times
over one "I give up"

Your soul is unbreakable,
no matter how broken it feels.

Your anger is not protecting you;
it's just causing you more pain.

Allow yourself to let go of the anger,
and feel the sadness.

Then let go,
and love.

I know it feels as if you are,
but you are not your pain,
your suffering, your ego,
your fear, your trauma.. you
are so much more.

It can never be broken,
your core.

The trauma did not make us stronger.
We made ourselves stronger
by adapting, by growing, by choosing..
second after second.. to keep going.

Time will move you along
and experience will heal you,
but you have to let go of the past
and the pain you are carrying
and take their hands.

There was a before and after.
I know I can't go back to the "before".
But I want to see what comes after the "after".

After the pain, after the healing.

We fantasize about who we used to be
and how we were before the bad things happened,
but we don't realize who we've become, how much
we've grown, and how much stronger we now are.

You have to let go of the past
so you can experience the present.
When you're stuck in the past,
time doesn't stand still; it just
moves on without you.

Does anyone else have songs that always comfort you whenever you hear them because you listened to them while going through times you weren't sure you'd be able to get through?

They remind you of all the pain you felt. But they also remind you that you made it through it, and you're stronger now than you ever were before.

How did you find
the words I felt
but could never explain..

How did you find them
hidden
under all this pain

How did you find
what I lived
but could never say

Are you ashamed..
you keep failing
over and over..
but you are over-
coming obstacles;
you are not failing.
You are learning.
You are growing.
Aren't you proud?

*Be with yourself
and no longer
will you feel alone.*

Maybe if we spent more time learning
how to love ourselves rather than
constantly trying to change how we look
or beating ourselves up
over not being "perfect",
we'd be happier.

Stop worrying that things are
"too good to be true".

Focus your energy on being grateful
for the way everything is working out and
you will be so much happier.

His love for her filled her mind, body, and spirit, overpowering all of her thoughts of how awfully inadequate she was. She no longer felt as if she was being torn apart. She felt as if all the broken pieces were being put back together.

As he embraced her, he made her feel whole again. As long as he held on, she would never fall apart. But she thought, "what if he let go?"

She would crack, with no one there to put her back together.. and in that moment, she realized no one could complete her because she was already complete. She only felt incomplete from the thoughts tearing her up inside. Realizing this, she promised herself she would learn to love herself, to fill herself up with love, so she could finally feel complete all on her own without feeling as if she would fall apart if he let go.

Always remind yourself that it is not selfish to take care of yourself and to care about your happiness. People who are happy are more likely to reach out and help others because if you're in a good mood, it's a lot more likely you'll be able to help others feel good when they're around you. But if you're in a bad mood, you're probably not going to have it in you to help lift someone else up when you are down.

So never feel bad or guilty for taking care of yourself and your happiness. Help yourself first and then you will be able to help others.

I dreamt
of being
with you,

but now
my dreams
are about me.

It's not too good to be true. You've just been conditioned to believe you are not "good enough" and that you deserve less than you really do.

-Decondition yourself.

You're so full of joy tears start pouring out and it feels as if you're releasing all of the pain you've held inside for so long and finally allowing yourself to be happy.

She kept going
even when she wanted to give up
and she got to a point in her life
where she no longer had to use
sleep as an escape because
she was living her dreams.

Anything could happen.

-it's ironic how this thought used to fill me up with so much anxiety and now it fills me up with so much excitement.

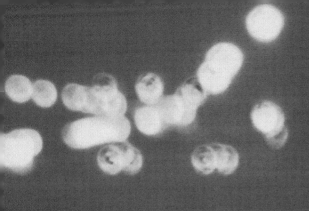

*Don't think of all the things
you haven't accomplished.
Think of all the things
you can accomplish
starting now.*

When you believe in yourself,
you will see obstacles as challenges
for you to overcome to reach your goals.

But when you don't believe in yourself,
you will see obstacles as challenges
stopping you from achieving your dreams.

When I let go of the need for control over my life, I felt the most in control I've ever been. Because letting go of needing things to happen a certain way allowed me to be in control of my feelings.

– I could choose to be at peace no matter what came my way

Start over, every second, if you need to. Start over until you make your life into the life you've always wanted to live. Start over until your dominant thoughts are thoughts that make you feel good, not bad. Start over until you are present and alive and connected to each moment. Start over until you take yourself off of autopilot and finally take charge of your life.

–you can start over.

The thing about setbacks is you don't even have to see them as setbacks. You can see them as propellers because they motivate you to work even harder because you don't ever want to feel like you did when you felt you were moving backwards instead of forward.

In this world, it's so easy to get used to something special. Don't let your thoughts distract you from what you feel. Don't let everyday life make you forget how it feels to be alive, how raindrops feel falling against your body, how music feels when it touches you and you can feel it in your bones, how moonlight on a summer night feels as you dance underneath it, how your loved ones make you feel, how it feels to fall in love with someone who you connect with so much you feel you've known them for eternities.

Don't ever let your mind make you forget what your soul feels like.

What makes you think that two humans can't take down their masks and uncover their souls, completely bare?

That two people can't cry, releasing all of the pain they've been enduring from the touch of a song in their ears. That a song can't go deeper, under your skin, touching your soul. Giving you a sense of relief like you are finally home.. and you're so happy love should be pouring out of you, but instead it's still tears. You can't explain it, but maybe the tears are making room for the happiness. Maybe the tears are helping you wash away all the pain you've been through. Maybe these tears are washing away everything you are not.. and maybe when you wipe your eyes, you will finally see yourself.

"You care too much about the world,"
she said.

"Or maybe you just care too little,"
he replied.

The people who will try to tell you
"one person won't make a difference"
are usually the ones who have gotten comfortable
with the way things are and don't want things to
change so they try to convince others or
themselves that one person cannot make a
difference. But that's a lie because all it takes is
one person to make a difference.

I promise I will love you, not only in those moments where you shine and finally feel as if you are "enough", but I will love you even in your darkest moments where you try to shut everyone out because you don't feel as if you deserve to be loved. *I promise.*

Maybe sometimes we have to
go through dark times
so we are forced to rekindle
the fire inside of us.

You've gotten so used to
focusing on all the things
that cause you pain
that you forgot about
everything that brings you joy.

What's hurting you doesn't have to hurt you so much. It doesn't have to take control of your life.

You can feel happiness again.

I will choose the happiness of this moment, instead of the pain of the past.

If someone ever says something to you
that is meant to hurt you, remember they
must be feeling really hurt themselves to try
to intentionally hurt another. This makes it
easier to have compassion for them, and if you
can't find compassion for them, at least be kind
to yourself and don't let their words get to you.

"Why do you care so much about
people you don't even know?" he asked.

"Because I can see myself in them..
and I want them to know they're not alone.
I know what it's like to want someone to see
your pain. Because if someone else sees it,
then you don't have to handle it all on your
own anymore. Then suddenly it's bearable..
and you don't feel so alone," she replied.

I can't explain how good it feels to trust
that your life is coming together, after
so many times of feeling as if it were
falling apart.

I used to dread the day
I would have to see you again.
But today I saw you, and I felt
unexpectedly happy..
because I no longer felt
anything toward you.

It no longer hurt to see you.

It's a great feeling to smile, the kind of smile that touches your eyes, the kind that almost hurts, the kind where you can't stop even if you tried because you're so genuinely happy to be alive in this moment. It's a great feeling to smile and finally feel as if you deserve to.. and it's sad that many of us feel as if we don't.

Let's unlearn feeling guilty for being happy.

You deserve friends who are happy for you when good things happen in your life. After you share good news with them, you should leave still feeling excited or maybe even more excited. But they shouldn't leave you feeling as if you had nothing to be excited for to begin with.

Friends should lift you up,

not bring you down.

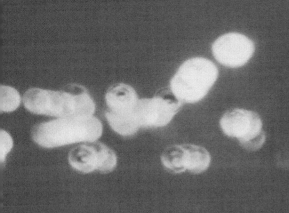

When he felt alone,
he would turn on
his favorite songs.

They surrounded him,
engulfed him
in a sea of warmth.

They embraced
his soul..
and he no longer
felt alone.

He fell in love with every part of you
you had been taught to hate,
and when you couldn't accept it
he sat down with you to wait

I'm learning how to stop being so afraid of "bad
emotions", how to stop being afraid to feel sad,
to feel angry, to feel hurt... how to stop being afraid
to feel. And ironically, it feels really good,
to allow myself to just be, to feel it all, without
feeling bad about it. Being human without feeling
guilty, as if I should always be happy or hide it if
I'm not. I'm learning how to just allow myself to
be, and I feel as if I'm finally

setting myself free.

Her goal was to love with her whole
heart without ending up feeling empty.

To be alone without feeling alone..

and to know she was still whole
even when she felt broken.

Our love is stronger than
what we are going through.

No matter how hard we try, we cannot recreate moments. That might be a sad thought, but at the same time, it's really beautiful.. because it means each moment is special and irreplaceable. Just like you and the people you spend it with.

-Cherish every moment.. and cherish the people you love. (I hope that includes yourself)

Try to be present in each moment.
Don't let life pass you by while
you are worrying about the future.

Think of someone in your life who you love with all of your heart. Do you look at that person with critical eyes and disgust, picking out their every "flaw"? Or do you just love and appreciate that person for who they are?

Think of all the people you love. Do you spend your time constantly picking them apart and hating them? No, because you are too busy loving them unconditionally.

You are so gentle, so kind, and so accepting with the people you love, but what about yourself? Don't be so hard on yourself. Make sure all of that love you extend is reaching you too.

Remember to love yourself as unconditionally as you love others.

You would never judge someone's worth based on their appearance, so why do you do it to yourself?

– you are so much more than your physical appearance

When you cannot see the beauty in yourself, think about this: Have you ever seen the beauty in others? The beauty of someone's compassion? Their kindness? Their acceptance? The beauty of someone's smile? Their laughter? Their carefree spirit? Have you ever seen the beauty in the world around you? The beauty of a sunny day, a rainy day, a sunset, a sunrise? The beauty of the leaves in the fall or a butterfly soaring by?

All of this beauty that you see, that you perceive, this beauty is also in you. All of it. You would not be able to perceive all of this beauty, if it didn't also exist within yourself. You may not see it now, but next time you notice the beauty of someone or something, appreciate it and remind yourself that this beauty, this light, this radiance is also within you.

I felt so lost and tired, struggling to find myself again.. and I realized maybe I wasn't meant to find who I used to be. Maybe I was meant to "lose myself" so I could be the person I've always wished I had the courage to be.

Hype will come and go. It won't ever last,
but self-worth, that's something you can always have.. being
enough, that's something you already are.. and loved, that's
something
you will always be.

Please don't let numbers and outside validation
ever determine your worth.

Your worth is incomparable to all of that.

He began to love himself again, and he realized he wasn't afraid of being alone because he no longer hated the person he was with. He now found comfort in being alone.

-because he had found love for himself.

One day you might feel differently.
You might wish you could go back
to the way things were between us.
You'll look for me, but I won't be
where you left me.

- and I won't be looking back

Spend this week cleansing. Clean and reorganize your room so that the atmosphere makes you feel good. Clean out your closet and donate anything you don't wear anymore, delete all the songs on your playlist that you always skip, clean out your photo album on your phone to make room to capture new memories. Delete old texts. Get rid of anything that reminds you of memories you would rather forget. Don't hold onto anything out of fear. Cleanse your mind of thoughts that make you doubt yourself and make you feel that you aren't good enough. Cleanse until you feel the clutter that was weighing you down has been washed away.

–*it's time for a fresh start.*

She wasn't looking for anyone at the moment..
because she was still looking for herself.

..and I won't tell you,
"please don't ever change"
because we are constantly
changing and growing.

But I will tell you,
"please don't ever change
for someone else"

The sun sets every single day, yet each day, you stare at it in wonder. It takes your breath away and fills your heart with a love you can't explain. Have you ever thought what if someone looks at you the same way?

What if you are someone's sunset?

I was whole before I knew him.
I was whole when I was with him.
..and I would still be whole without him.

-you are complete already.
Share your completeness with one another
instead of trying to find someone
outside of yourself to complete you.

I thought I would be sad when I found out he didn't want me, but I surprised myself. I felt so happy and free as I drove away. I can't believe that I've grown this much that I actually love myself enough to set myself free. Free from needing someone else to love me in order for me to love myself. I wanted him, but I didn't need him and that felt liberating.

- I am free

Everything was working out just as I had always wanted it to, and I started to feel knots churning in my stomach because I felt as if everything was too good to be true. I was scared I would wake up to find it had all been a dream because it had to be. Seriously, how could this be real? How could I deserve this? I remember thinking about all of the people I've hurt in the past and wondered how I could ever forgive myself for what I've done even though I never meant to hurt them.

If I could go back, I would do things differently. If I knew what I knew now, I would never have done what I did in the past. I'm not the same as I was back then..

and that's when I realized, maybe I can forgive myself. Maybe I can't forgive the person who hurt people in the past, but I am a different person now. And the person I am now would never do the same things that I did in the past because I know better now.

-So maybe the person I am today deserves to be forgiven.

Have you ever been friends with someone for a long time and then one day you realize you've fallen in love with them?

Maybe that's how you need to fall in love with yourself. Maybe you need to become your own friend first, by being kinder to yourself and caring about your happiness and telling yourself things that will lift you up instead of tear you down.

-I hope you will stop being your own worst enemy and become friends with yourself. I hope, one day, you will see yourself in a new light.. and one day, I hope you find that you've fallen in love with yourself.

Don't edit yourself around people. Know that you are good enough as you are. Don't feel pressured to put up an image of being perfect. Free yourself from the fear of not being accepted and allow yourself to be seen, truly, genuinely seen. This is the only way to find people who will love you for who you are and not what you pretend to be. *This is the only way to truly connect with others.*

I know there are people in your life that you love with everything that you are. You love them so much you can't even imagine life without them they're the ones you believe are worth living for, but you need to learn to love yourself as much as you love them because if something were to ever happen to the people you love, you'll need a reason to keep going. You need to believe you are worth living for too.

-You need to be one of the people that you love.

..but I don't think I can go back to who I was..
and maybe that's not a bad thing. I've changed.
But maybe that's a good thing. I miss who I used
to be, but I am starting to learn how to love who
I have become.. and I am starting to
take care of myself again.

Don't listen to those who tell you success is more important than your happiness. Success means different things to different people. Would you call yourself successful if you were living a life that didn't make you happy?

You're here for a reason and your life matters.
I know it can be hard, but imagine what you want
your life to be like and think of the future and how
happy you'll be because it really does get better.

Keep going and it will be worth
all this pain you've endured.

Are you in love?

Not romantically,
but in love with yourself, life,
waking up in the morning,
smiling, laughing, crying,
growing through life
one second at a time,

going through hardships
and still loving life..

Remember to celebrate your loved ones every single day. Remember to not only show your love for them on birthdays, holidays, and anniversaries. Express how you feel through your words and actions daily. *Take the time to remember.*

Do you check on your phone
more often than you check on
the person sitting beside you?

Don't take each other for granted.

Even on the days you don't feel worthy of love, they will show you so much love.

–they will remind you you're worthy of all the love in the world, unconditionally.

I know this moment won't last forever,
but this moment is enough.

It is all I need.

I realized I do have a right to feel upset,
but next time I want to remember I also
have the right to choose to feel happy,
to let it go and be happy.

I will not let all the pain I feel
make me forget all the love I have.

Pay attention to the people in your life.
Make sure they've actually gotten better
and not just better at hiding it.
Remind them they are not a burden.
Help them remember they are loved.

There are still loyal people in this world. There are people who would never dream of hurting you. There are people you can trust. Keep believing this, no matter how many times you've been hurt, and you will find people who still know how to love.

Don't stop believing in love just because you've met people who didn't know how to.

Transform your pain
into understanding..
and then love

How to be happier

1. Place your happiness back into your own hands.

2. Allow yourself to feel "negative" emotions, such as sadness, anger, etc. but do not hold onto those feelings; let them go.

3. Allow yourself to feel happy, but don't hold on so tightly to it. don't be afraid that if you let go, you won't be able to find it again. You don't need to search for happiness, happiness lives in your soul. And it waits for your mind to let it in, to allow yourself to feel it.

You can make a difference.

Don't ever let anyone tell you that you can't.

Find your passion and what makes you come alive because your life does have meaning. You can have many passions, but if you haven't found what you're passionate about yet, and you don't know what your "purpose" is just become passionate about your life and living it to the fullest, and you will still make a difference. Don't worry about finding your "purpose". Maybe your purpose is just to learn to love and appreciate yourself, others, and life.. and by doing this, you help inspire others to do the same.

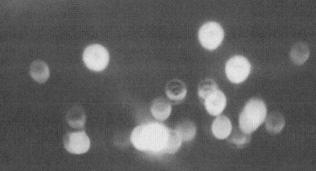

All they had
was love
but they felt
as if they had it all.

They lived for those moments
that took their breath away,
where their hearts
beat faster
as their breath
slowed
to a
crawl.

Don't be afraid to tell them how you feel. Or be afraid, be completely scared.. but do it anyway! Do it even if your voice trembles and your hands shake and your heart feels like it's going to stop beating right as you begin to speak. Do it.. if you know that if you don't, you'll look back with regret, wondering *"What if.."*

And now I understand we had to wait to become who we are now, before we could meet. If we had met a moment too soon, we would've been meeting entirely different people.. and we might not have connected in the way we are now.

You are enough.
You are not lacking anything,
except for confidence in yourself.

I think we all go through phases and it's normal to feel different emotions, but it's possible to get to a point in your life where you're happy more often than you are sad, a point in your life where if someone asked if you were okay you would be able to say yes and actually mean it.

Are you doing what your soul desires?
Or are you doing things to distract yourself
from what you truly desire?

Night Sky

Why wait for a new year
to start a new beginning?
Why even wait for a new day?
What's wrong with
the here and now?

No more excuses.

Start living the life
you've always wanted.

Why wait to live?

Live now.

Be the reason you get up every morning.
You are worth living for.

People often talk about how much a year can change things, but one day can change a lot too. It's crazy how quickly some things can change.

– One day can change a lot.
The next time you feel like giving up,
remember that.

Life is so surreal. In a week or a month,
your entire life could be different.
Things that you once only dreamed of
could actually be your reality.

One day you're going to be sitting in a car on a road trip with people you love or on your way to the beach or a party or a place you've never been. You'll have the windows down and you'll feel the wind against your skin and the music in your bones. You'll all be dancing and singing along to your favorite songs, but once you see that you're about to pass through a tunnel, you'll all stop so you can hold your breath and make a wish once you've made it out. But midway through the tunnel, you'll realize there is nothing you can wish for because in this moment, you already feel as if you have everything you've ever wanted. And you'll let out a breath and laugh as you realize how perfect everything is, making everyone else break down laughing too and you'll all keep driving through the tunnel, the thought of wishing for more completely gone from your mind because in this moment, you feel as if you have it all.

You feel alive and you feel as if being alive is finally enough.

Little by little, day by day,
you work towards where
you want to be...
and one day, it happens so soon,
it seems surreal you are where
you once dreamed you'd be.

Change your mindset from "I cannot do that" to "one day, I will be able to do that!"

Sometimes you're not lacking anything except patience.

Some say that if you really, truly want something then you will work towards it every single day, otherwise your heart isn't really set on obtaining it.

But if you find that you truly do want something with all your heart, but aren't working towards it, maybe it's because you are afraid of getting what you've always desired. Maybe a part of you doesn't think you deserve it, or you're afraid once you get it, it will be taken away from you.. whatever the reason is, find a way to work through it, so that it doesn't stop you from going after what you really want. You do deserve it, but it won't matter what anyone else says until you believe it.

Lose your fears and gain
what you've always wanted.

We can put limits on ourselves
or we can put in the work daily
and see what new possibilities
we can discover.

If it's important to you,
keep trying no matter how many times
you feel like you have to start over.

Trust the timing of your life,
but don't let your life pass you by;
do the work.

Keep healing and growing and learning.

What if living our dreams meant working towards our dreams, but being present for every second of our lives, being grateful for every second we get to live in our bodies, being filled with contentment and love? Wouldn't we be living our dreams today? Instead of waiting for some future date?

Never let anyone become your universe.
You are your own universe. There is something
extraordinarily beautiful when you share your
universe with another, when two come together
to create an entirely new cosmos to explore,
but remember to never lose yourself.

Connect, explore, grow, and amidst all of the
adventure, find pieces of yourself you never
knew existed, but never lose yourself.

You deserve a love so strong
and a connection so deep
you will never have to question
whether it's real
because you will see it
in their eyes and feel it
in your soul.

I looked into your eyes
and I saw
they held my soul

Why don't we start asking each other meaningful questions.. like how did you learn to love and accept yourself? In which ways are you living your dreams? How did you discover what makes you truly happy? Instead of constantly asking questions that make us focus so much on the external like what brand are you wearing?

Questions that make us forget what's inside.

Forgetting who we are.

Hopes

I don't know if anyone has ever told you this before, but you are important. You matter. I hope this isn't the first time you've been told this. But if it is, I hope you know that you were always important and you always mattered even if no one ever told you. (I hope you remember that).

I hope you know that you should never have to feel sorry for not being something someone else wants you to be. If they try to make you feel bad or guilty for being yourself, they don't love you, they love an idea of you.

I hope you end up living the life of your dreams. I hope you wake up every morning with a fire in your soul that you won't ever let anyone put out.. and I hope when you lay your head down to sleep at night, instead of crying yourself to sleep, you will finally be the kind of happy you always wished you could be.

A promise

Please remember you are not alone.
Please remember you are loved.
Please remember your life makes a difference.
And please, please remember that your smile
alone could light up the entire world.

Promise me you'll remember.

The world needs your light.

Self-care is important

Nourish your body
Examples: Make a slushy, smoothie, or ice cream out of some of your favorite fruits – make a salad – make a guacamole bowl – experiment with making something new that's healthy but also extremely delicious

Stay active
Example: Do your favorite workouts – go running – go hiking – dance

Read
examples: - read inspiring books – reread your favorite books – read uplifting quotes

Write
examples: - write down quotes that mean something to you so that you can read them later when you need something to keep you going – write down things you're grateful for – write down your goals – write down the everyday things you can do to work towards achieving your goals

Self-care is important (cont.)

Other examples: -find new songs -make a playlist of soul songs and then dance as if this moment is all that matters, as if this moment will last forever -lie down and listen to music with your headphones while just breathing in and out, being in the moment and being grateful for being alive – play an instrument -take a relaxing shower at night or when the sun is setting so you can shower with the window open and feel as if you are living in a dream because the sunset or night sky is so breathtaking and when you're done, look out the window close your eyes and feel the breeze against your face, taking a moment to be present, feeling grateful you are able to experience this very moment. -go out hiking or for a walk -do whatever you need to do, to take care of yourself *you deserve to love yourself enough to take care of yourself*

The feeling you have deep down is right. Your life does matter and you were meant to do incredible things in this life. It may be deep-rooted, forgotten through your years in this world, but if you dig deep enough, you can feel it.

Deep down, you already know this.

Healing from heartbreak

-feel the pain, don't be ashamed of it or afraid to feel it.

-allow yourself to grieve, but don't allow yourself to become consumed by it. It's just a feeling, and not who you are, and definitely not how you will feel the rest of your life.

-we feel our heart can be broken because it's the way we perceive our love while in human bodies, but when we realize we are love and our love is limitless because we are made of it, we realize we are unbroken. Our souls can never be broken.

-but, we are in human bodies right now, and sometimes we feel the pain so much that we can't take it, so we have to remind ourselves that this feeling is not who we are and find ways to feel close to our soul again.

Healing from heartbreak (cont.)

-we do this by doing things that make us feel happy and alive; if you don't know what that is, have fun exploring and finding what that is

-one thing that we can all do to feel closer to our soul is simply to be present. It sounds so simple, but for a lot of us it can be a challenge because our thoughts won't allow us to be.

-and remember, every time you go through something that makes you feel weak, you are actually becoming stronger. You are healing, but at the same time, you are also growing.

...don't break others
because others tried
to break you.

Break the cycle...
and the healing
can begin.

If you've been cheated on or hurt badly
by someone you loved, and you want proof
you can meet someone who would never dream
of hurting you and who would love you...

You.

You are the proof.
The way you loved them
with everything that you are.
The way you were honest and loyal
and gentle and always there.
You are proof a love that is
out of this world still exists.
You know it's real.
You know it exists.
It's you.

You feel as if your life has just begun..
and in a way, it has.
This is the life you've always wanted;
you are finally allowing yourself to live it,
and it has just begun.

Feelings of happiness come and go
but love is always there

Maybe it has felt that each day has gotten harder and now you're wondering why anyone would ever say "it gets better with time." **But it does get better.** For some of us, it will feel as if each day, the pain is taking over, but from working through the pain, there will come a day where you get a glimpse of your future self and for the first time in a long time, you can picture yourself happy.. **and each day, it will get a little easier, as love starts to take over.** Everything will feel brand new. You'll look at the sky and the trees and the ocean and wonder if everything always looked this vibrant and alive. Maybe it had, but your mind wouldn't let you see it.. **and each day, you'll feel a little bit lighter, as the pain that was weighing you down starts leaving your body.** You'll feel as if anything is possible, as if the sky is at your fingertips.. **and before you know it, you will be the person you caught a glimpse of when you wondered if things would ever get better.. and you will be at peace**

– happier than you ever imagined.

Thank you.

Thank you, for being here.

*If you are reading this, I wanted
to thank you for holding a space
for me to share this with you.*

*Thank you to every single person reading this,
and thank you to every single person in my
life. Thank you so much for everything. Thank
you so much for your help, support,
encouragement, and your love.*

*And thank you to my husband, Josue
who told everyone I was going to write books,
before I even thought I could.*

**If you're from my social media, and want the
same feeling as my videos you can go to my
Spotify for night drive playlists to listen to
while reading this book: @samxcamargo*

Made in the USA
Las Vegas, NV
03 January 2021